Scary Creatures
of the
RAIN FOREST

Written by
Penny Clarke

FRANKLIN WATTS
An Imprint of Scholastic Inc.
NEW YORK • TORONTO • LONDON • AUCKLAND • SYDNEY
MEXICO CITY • NEW DELHI • HONG KONG
DANBURY, CONNECTICUT

Created and designed
by David Salariya

Author:

Penny Clarke is an author and editor specializing in nonfiction books for children. She has written books on natural history, rain forests, and volcanoes, as well as books on various periods in history. She used to live in central London, but thanks to modern technology she has now realized her dream of being able to live and work in the countryside.

Artists:

John Francis

Robert Morton

Carolyn Scrace

Nicholas Hewetson

Terry Riley

Mark Bergin

Shirley Willis

Lizzie Harper

Series Creator:

David Salariya was born in Dundee, Scotland. In 1989 he established The Salariya Book Company. He has illustrated a wide range of books and has created many new series for publishers in the U.K. and overseas. He lives in Brighton, England, with his wife, illustrator Shirley Willis, and their son.

Editor: Stephen Haynes

Editorial Assistants:
Rob Walker, Tanya Kant

Picture Research:
Mark Bergin, Carolyn Franklin

Photo Credits:

t=top, b=bottom

Tom Brakefield/Verve: 15b, 18, 22, 25
Cadmium: 8, 15t
John Foxx Images: 12
Mountain High Maps/© 1993 Digital
    Wisdom Inc.: 6–7
Photodisc: 4
PhotoSpin Inc.: 11

PAPER FROM
SUSTAINABLE
FORESTS

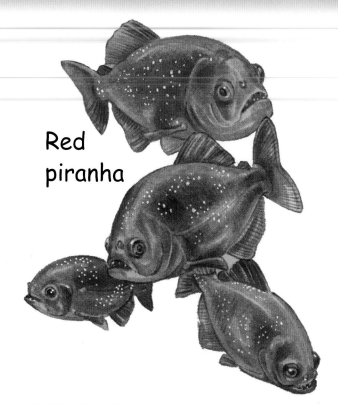

Red piranha

Created, designed, and produced by
The Salariya Book Company Ltd
Book House
25 Marlborough Place
Brighton BN1 1UB

A CIP catalog record for this title is available from the Library of Congress.

ISBN-13: 978-0-531-20544-0 (Lib. Bdg.)
              978-0-531-21010-9 (Pbk.)
ISBN-10: 0-531-20544-4 (Lib. Bdg.)
              0-531-21010-3 (Pbk.)

Published in the United States by Franklin Watts
An Imprint of Scholastic Inc.
557 Broadway
New York, NY 10012

Printed in China.

Contents

Goliath beetle

What is a Rain Forest?

This book is about **tropical** rain forests. Forests grow all over the world, but different types of plants grow in different conditions and climates. Plants in tropical rain forests need at least 80 inches (200 cm) of rain that falls evenly throughout the year and an almost constant temperature of 79° Fahrenheit (26°C). Only tropical regions of the world have these conditions.

Tropical rain forests are richer in plants and animals than anywhere else on Earth. Most rain forest trees are very tall, growing to about 165 feet (50 m), but a few reach 200 feet (60 m). These huge trees provide different **habitats** for the thousands of **species** living in rain forests.

Emerald tree boa

Emerald tree boas kill by wrapping themselves around and choking their **prey.**

Emerald
tree boa

Heliconid
butterfly

Topaz
hummingbird

Red-eyed tree frog

Poison arrow
frog

Leaf-cutter ant

Where Are the Rain Forests?

You'll find tropical rain forests in South and Central America, Africa, and Southeast Asia. They grow only in tropical lowlands because those regions have the perfect climate for tropical rain forests.

Anacondas are snakes that crush their prey.

Anaconda

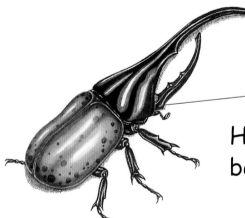

Hercules beetle

Common caiman

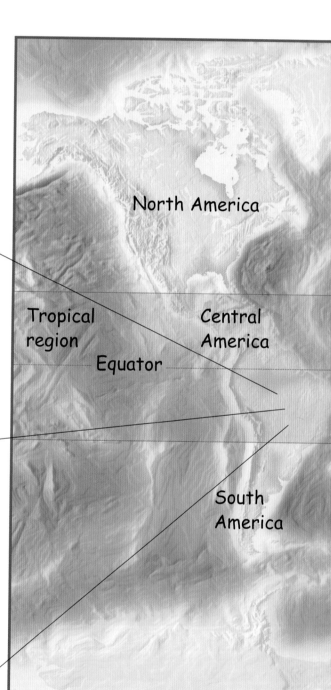

North America

Tropical region

Central America

Equator

South America

Caimans live in the rivers of the Amazon rain forest.

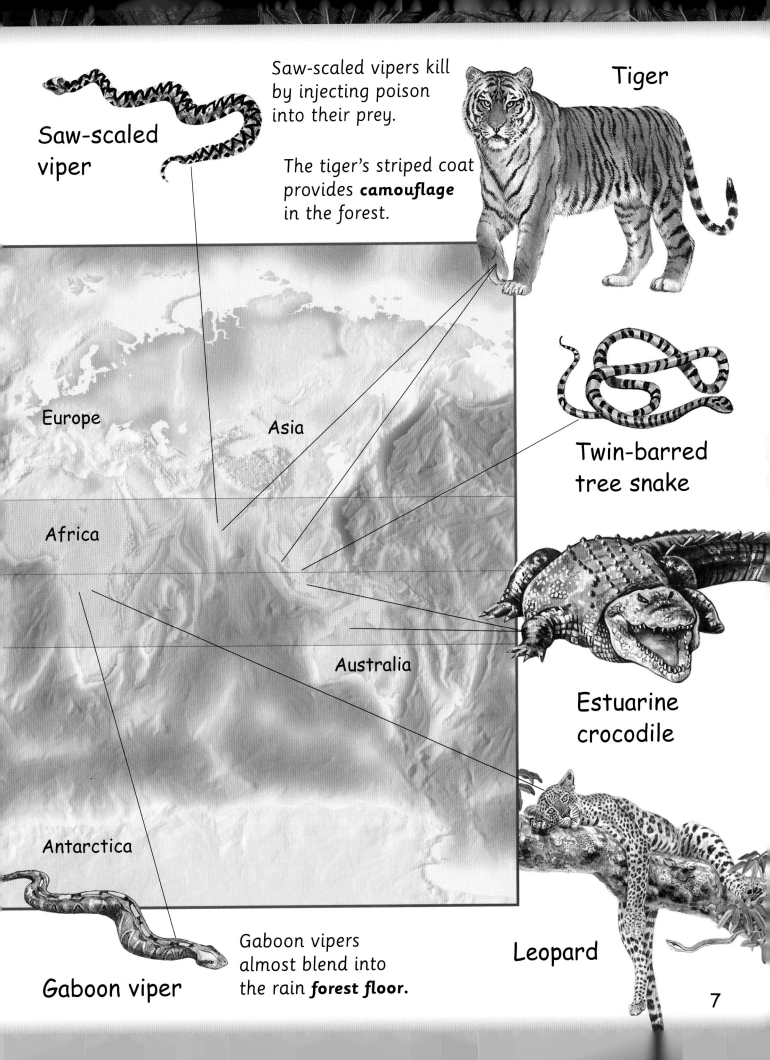

Saw-scaled
viper

Saw-scaled vipers kill
by injecting poison
into their prey.

The tiger's striped coat
provides **camouflage**
in the forest.

Tiger

Europe

Asia

Twin-barred
tree snake

Africa

Australia

Estuarine
crocodile

Antarctica

Gaboon viper

Gaboon vipers
almost blend into
the rain **forest floor.**

Leopard

7

Did You Know?

In a rain forest more plants grow
on the trees than on the ground!

What Is Interdependence?

Every habitat is the home of many different species. Take away one species, and some others would not survive because each one depends on several others. This is called interdependence. Rain forest trees provide homes for hundreds of animals, but the trees depend on the animals, too.

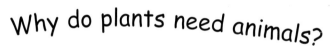
Why do plants need animals?

Plants need insects to **pollinate** their flowers. They need birds and other animals to spread their seeds by eating their fruit.

Scientists estimate that every 2.5 acres (1 hectare) of tropical rain forest has about 750 species of trees, 1,500 other species of plants, and 42,000 species of insects—and that's not counting all the birds, reptiles, amphibians, and **mammals**!

Pitcher plant

Pitcher plants trap insects in their "pitchers."

Keel-billed toucan

Cotton-topped
tamarin

Red-
faced
uakari

Saw-billed hermit
hummingbird

Woolly
monkey

Pierid
butterfly

Did You Know?

Scientists divide rain forests into five layers. From the top down these are: **emergent layer** (the tops of the very tallest trees), **canopy** (the tops of most trees), **understory** (short, young trees), **shrub layer** (bushes), and **forest floor**.

Are Rain Forests Dark and Scary?

It depends where you are. Rain forest trees are so tall and have such thick, leafy tops that little light reaches the ground. So at ground level it is very dark, but in the treetops it is light.

Tarantulas look much more scary than they are. They feed on insects, young birds, lizards, and frogs.

Meeting a jaguar in the rain forest would be very scary!

Tarantula

What Lives in the Canopy?

Because the canopy is bright and sunny, more creatures live there than anywhere else in the rain forest. Brilliantly colored birds and butterflies dart about in the canopy, feeding on the bright flowers and fruit.

X-Ray Vision

Hold the next page up to the light to see some of the creatures that live in the rain forest canopy.

See what's inside

Birds' beaks tell you what they eat. Hummingbirds have long, thin beaks to reach nectar deep inside flowers. Macaws (right) crack open nuts with their small, tough beaks. Toucans (below) pick fruit with their long, curved beaks.

Toucan

Macaw

Toucans also grab eggs from other birds' nests with their big beaks.

The trees of the canopy are not the tallest in the forest. A few even taller ones soar above them. These are the "forest giants" of the emergent layer, so named because they emerge from the rest of the rain forest.

Harpy eagle

Macaw

Hummingbird

Morpho butterfly

Howler monkey

Squirrel monkey

Three-toed sloth

Do Monkeys Live in the Rain Forest?

Yes! Wherever there are rain forests, there are monkeys. The calls of the howler monkey echo across the forest. Squirrel monkeys scamper through the canopy and into the emergent layer, where danger may hover as a harpy eagle flies overhead. But the greatest threat is loss of habitat as rain forests are felled.

Squirrel monkey

Squirrel monkeys live in the South American rain forest. They use their long tails to help them balance as they jump from tree to tree searching for food.

Orangutans live only in the rain forests of Southeast Asia. They can use their powerful arms to swing through the trees, but they usually walk along branches (and on the ground) on all fours or upright.

Female orangutan with baby

Oasis hummingbird

Glass-wing butterfly

Postman butterfly

Tamandua with its young

Coati

Nine-banded armadillo

Up or Down?

Even though scientists divide the rain forest into layers, many animals travel from one layer to another. For example, the tamandua, or tree anteater, lives mainly above the forest floor feeding on ants, but it comes down to the ground if it discovers a termite nest.

Did You Know?

About 50 different species of ant live in the South American rain forest alone. Ants are very good climbers.

Most birds and butterflies live near the canopy, where it is warm and sunny. But when a giant forest tree comes crashing down, light floods into the lower levels and butterflies and birds start living here—until the trees grow and shut out the light again.

Larger mammals live mainly on the forest floor, although some, like leopards and jaguars, are good climbers. Large packs of the ground-dwelling South American coati forage for insects, spiders, lizards, and fruit.

Goliath beetle

African goliath beetles are about 4 inches (10 cm) long. Adults live in the canopy, but the females fly down to lower layers to lay their eggs.

Can Worms Really Live Up in the Air?

Yes, they can! Scientists have found worms in crevices of tree trunks many feet above the forest floor. Leaves fall into these crevices. The worms eat the leaves and turn them into compost, just as they would on the ground. Perhaps their eggs were carried on the feet of ants climbing up and down the tree trunks.

Did You Know?
Some rain forest frogs defend themselves by **secreting** poison through their skins. This poison is strong enough to kill humans.

Red-eyed tree frog

The red-eyed tree frog is not poisonous.

The pike-headed vine snake eats lizards and young birds.

Pike-headed vine snake

Many plants on rain forest trees are **epiphytes**, which means that they grow on the trees but do not harm them. Because these plants contain the green pigment chlorophyll, they can make their own food from sunlight and rain.

Bromeliads are common rain forest plants. You may not have visited a rain forest, but you may have eaten a bromeliad. That cluster of sharp leaves is the clue. The answer? Pineapples are bromeliads!

Water forms pools at the base of bromeliad leaves. Tree frogs lay their eggs in these pools.

Bromeliad

Dragonfly

Skeleton butterfly

What Happens on the Forest Floor?

Many creatures living on rain forest floors are small but necessary. Without them there would be no rain forest trees and so no rain forests. Why? Because these creatures help provide **nutrients** for the rain forest's trees.

Animals on the rain forest floor provide the nutrients trees need to survive. These animals break down dead things and release their nutrients into the soil, where tree roots can absorb them.

 Did You Know?

In habitats all over the world, dung beetles carry out the essential task of clearing up animal dung.

Crescent-horned dung beetle

Male Hercules beetles can grow up to 6.5 inches (17 cm) long, but the beakless females are only 3.5 inches (9cm). They lay their eggs in fallen rain forest trees and their tunneling helps break down the trees.

Hercules beetle

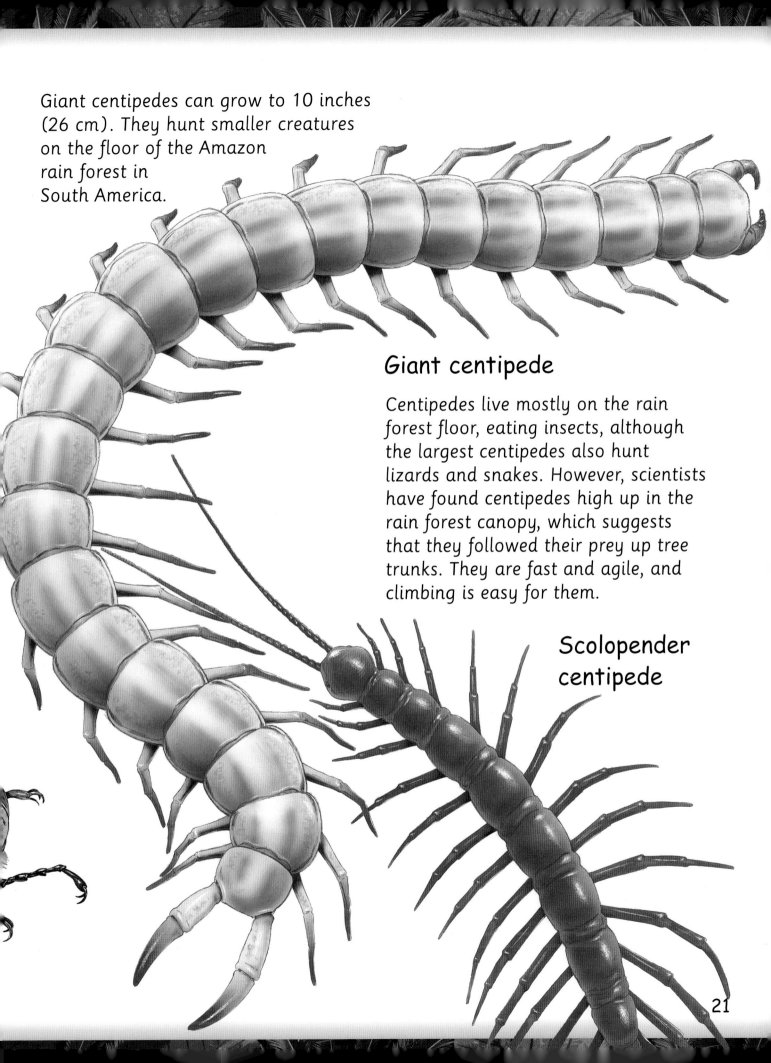

Giant centipedes can grow to 10 inches (26 cm). They hunt smaller creatures on the floor of the Amazon rain forest in South America.

Giant centipede

Centipedes live mostly on the rain forest floor, eating insects, although the largest centipedes also hunt lizards and snakes. However, scientists have found centipedes high up in the rain forest canopy, which suggests that they followed their prey up tree trunks. They are fast and agile, and climbing is easy for them.

Scolopender centipede

Are There Scary Creatures in the Rain Forest?

Yes, every habitat has scary creatures, because every habitat has fierce hunters and other dangerous animals. Not all these creatures are dangerous to humans, though. Cats like leopards and jaguars attack only if they feel threatened.

X-Ray Vision

Hold the next page up to the light to see more scary rain forest creatures.

See what's inside

Strawberry poison arrow frog

This tiny frog won't attack you, but it is still dangerous. It secretes a strong poison in self-defense. Native peoples of the South American rain forest use the poison on their weapons.

The leopard's spotted coat is good camouflage as the leopard stalks its prey or waits on a tree branch before dropping onto an antelope passing below.

Leopard

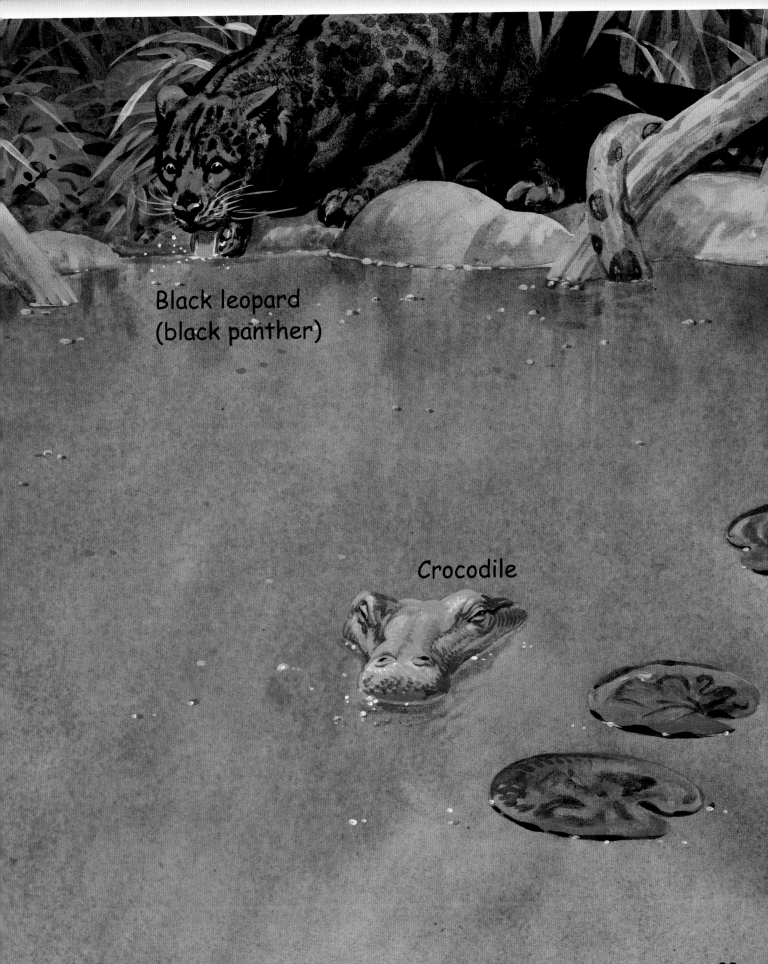

Black leopard
(black panther)

Crocodile

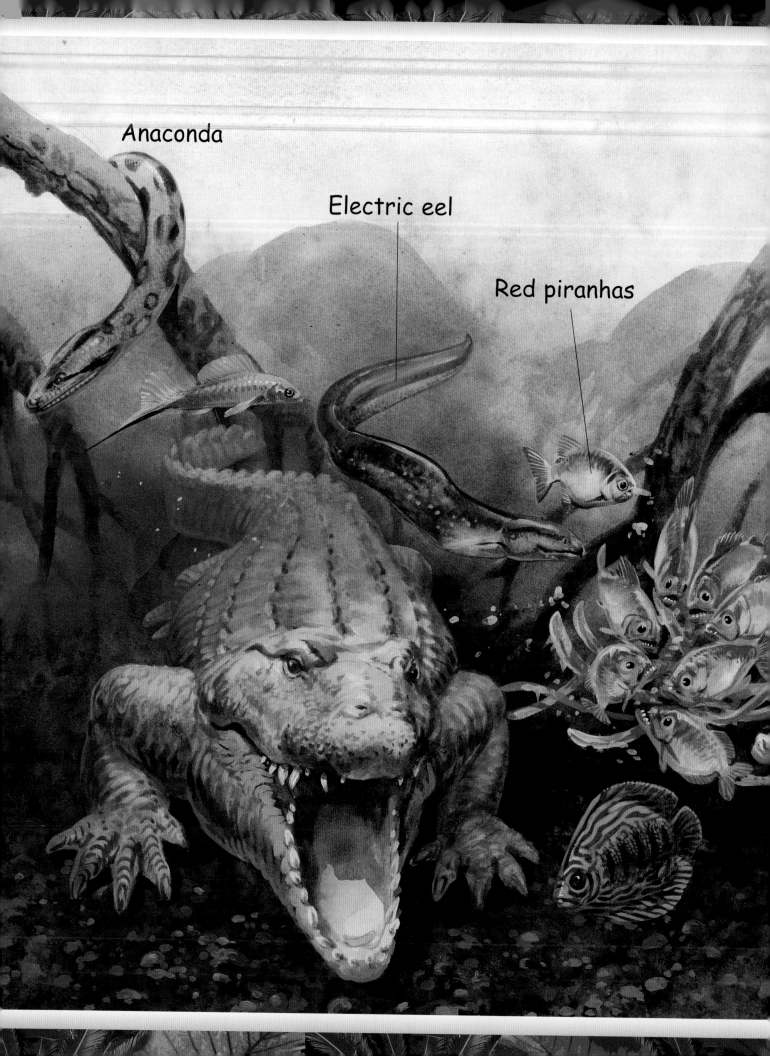

Anaconda

Electric eel

Red piranhas

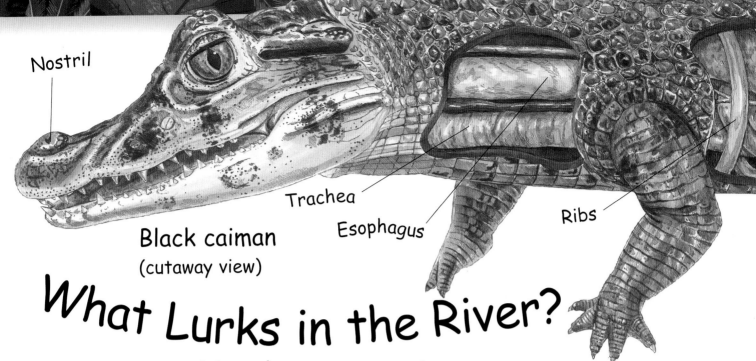

Nostril

Trachea

Esophagus

Ribs

Black caiman
(cutaway view)

What Lurks in the River?

Huge rivers, like the Amazon in South America and the Congo in Africa, flow through the rain forests. Sunlight floods in and the riverbanks are thick with vegetation. Many unique creatures live in the rivers and along the banks.

"Kill or be killed" applies everywhere in the rain forest, even in the rivers. River **predators** include members of the crocodile family, such as the black caiman of the Amazon and the estuarine crocodile of Southeast Asia.

Electric eels stun their prey with an electric current. Anacondas lurk on the riverbank, waiting to kill animals coming to drink. But killers don't always win. A school of piranhas (opposite) is eating what the crocodile has just killed.

Crocodile

Poison-tipped arrow

Yanomami village

Yanomami hunter

In the Amazon rain forest the Yanomami people built communal houses called *malocas*. Every few years they would move on and build another.

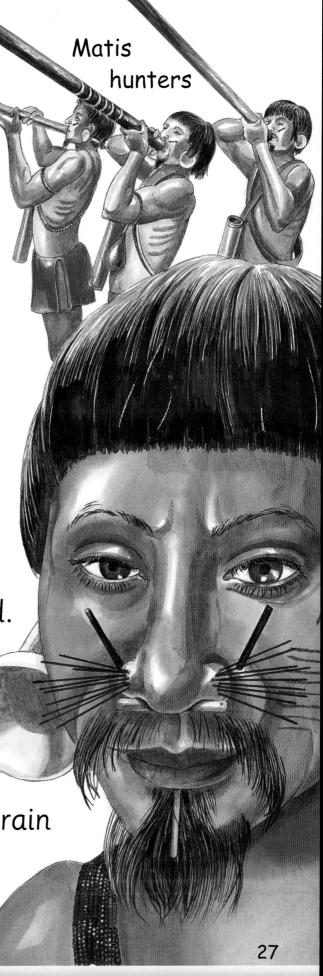

Matis hunters

Do People Live in Rain Forests?

Rain forests used to be good places for people to live. The forest was so rich in fruits, seeds, and nuts that growing crops was unnecessary. People just collected what they needed. The men hunted using blowpipes with darts or bows and arrows. They dipped the tips of their darts or arrows in poison from poison arrow frogs. But as the rain forest has disappeared, so has this way of life. Few people live in this way today.

Are Rain Forests in Danger?

Sadly, the answer is "Yes." All rain forests and the living things they support are in danger. Many countries with rain forests are poor. Some people there think of rain forests as wasted space because crops aren't being grown.

Searching for oil destroys rain forests but brings companies millions of dollars.

Endangered tiger

Rain forest peoples used to make medicines from the forest plants. Destroying the forests and their peoples destroys this knowledge. Fortunately, knowledge of the rosy periwinkle from Madagascar was not lost—it is now used in some cancer treatments.

Using renewable rain forest resources, such as latex (rubber), could help rain forests survive.

Shaman making medicine

Did You Know?

Scientists have determined that rain forest trees release 22 billion tons (20 billion tonnes) of water into the Earth's atmosphere every day. With no rain forests to do this, there would be much less rainfall around the world.

Quetzal

Rain Forest Facts

Malaria, a disease that can kill humans, is spread by mosquitoes. Quinine, the first treatment for malaria, was made from the bark of the cinchona tree from the South American rain forest.

Rubber is made from the sap of a tree that first grew in the Amazon rain forest.

All mammals breathe in oxygen and breathe out carbon dioxide. Trees and plants, on the other hand, absorb carbon dioxide. Cutting down rain forests will mean that less carbon dioxide can be absorbed. Scientists think that too much carbon dioxide in the atmosphere will increase global warming.

Birds of paradise live only in the Asian rain forests. The forests are so dense that no one is sure how many species there are.

The three-toed sloth moves very, very slowly. It has special grooved hairs in its coat in which green algae grow. They help camouflage the sloth by making it look like the leafy branches among which it lives.

Once an area of rain forest has been cut down, it can never grow again. No longer protected by vegetation, the thin soil is soon washed or blown away.

Many rain forest trees have two kinds of roots: ordinary roots and buttress roots. Buttress roots grow down the outside of a tree's trunk and into the ground. Without these, the tree would not be able to support itself in the shallow rain forest soil.

If you want to help the rain forests, you can support environmental organizations and learn as much as you can about the rain forest and its wildlife. Try to avoid buying anything that might have come from a rain forest. This could be a bird or some other animal (jewelry made from butterflies' wings has been fashionable in the past)—or something made from rain forest wood. And always ignore anyone who tells you that one person's action won't make any difference.

Glossary

camouflage Special markings or coloring on an animal that help it to blend in with its surroundings.

canopy The layer of the rain forest where the tops of most of the trees are.

emergent layer The tops of the tallest trees in the rain forest.

endangered In danger of dying out.

epiphyte A plant that grows on other plants (mostly trees) without harming them. Epiphytes get the water they need not through their roots but from rain trapped in their leaves.

forest floor The lowest level of the rain forest.

habitat The place where a particular type of plant or animal lives naturally.

mammal A hairy or furry animal that feeds on its mother's milk when it is young.

nutrient A substance that gives nourishment.

pollinate To exchange pollen between flowering plants. If its flowers are not pollinated, a plant cannot produce its fruit or seeds.

predator An animal that hunts other animals for food.

prey An animal that is hunted for food.

secrete To produce or give off a substance.

shaman A wise man or healer in a native tribe.

shrub layer The second-lowest level of the forest, where shrubs and small trees grow.

species A group of plants or animals that look alike, live in the same way, and produce young that do the same.

White-tailed deer

tropical Belonging to the tropics—the part of the Earth that is between the Tropic of Cancer north of the Equator and the Tropic of Capricorn south of the Equator. This area has the warmest climate on Earth.

understory The level of the rain forest where the younger and shorter trees are.

Index